BLEEDING BETWEEN THE BARS

Written by Da'Juan ''DonJuan'' Carter-Woodard

CONTENT

PREFACE

1. ISOLATION CELL
2. THESE WALLS SPEAK
3. GO
4. SILENCE SPEAKS SO LOUD
5. EDIBLE AUCTION BLOCK
6. R U READY
7. FORGIVENESS
8. MIGHTIER THEN THE SWORD
9. INNER ARTIST
10. WARRIOR MINDSET
11. TIME
12. PREPPING MY PEOPLE
13. TIME (PASSING US BY)
14. LOVE MEANT FOR YOU
15. WAKE UP
16. IN THIS ROOM
17. HEALTH CARE
18. UPPER D MEN
19. NO REMORSE
20. CHRISTMAS BLUES

PREFACE

This is a piece composed of things I wrote while incarcerated. I feel it was important for me to take my

time and turn it into something positive and productive. So many times we find our words in silence.

Most of our genius moments are in the place where we feel the most alone. For me, this was my time

alone, away from my kids and family. So with this I dedicate this to them. My Kids that I love, Jameela

Monae, Za`Niyah Amira, Julian Nathaniel, Keyon Maceo, Zakee and Jahreea. To my Mother Diane aka

Lady D who was there thru it all. For my Sibling Tee James, one of the strongest people I know. Also for

my Father Terry who tried his best to understand me and be a source of support when needed. To my

Family at Eastside Arts Alliance for their constant support and love. This is a book with stories that may

ring bells in many people lives. A tale of so many that is heard by so few. Here is my contribution to all

the brothers and sisters and children that live between these wall throughout America. These are stories

meant to be heard. My story may not match them all, but the message of self reflection and police

repression should be clear. Thank you to all that support this book. Now, if you will, TAKE A RIDE WITH

ME THROUGH THE OTHER SIDE

where we are Bleeding Between These Bars.

Isolation Cell

What makes your respect more than mine?

Is it your title you hold so dearly to?

Or the fact you think the only way to respect you

Is to belittle myself

Over compensation because of fear

Makes you push extra hard

Intimidated by my size, my stature, my confidence

To where you feel we can't meet eye to eye

Maybe it's the fact you had a bad day

Or the lack of respect you receive at home

Bringing a chip on your shoulder to your workplace

Insecure enough to think we can see your weakness

So out of control you fight to keep control

What better place to assert your authority

Then with inmates

But when dealing with convicts

Some of them view respect as a form of survival

And respect is a 2-way street

Cutting corners and striking deals

To piece together a common ground

But when you have nothing to barter with

The ground crumbles beneath your

feet

Life is a game of give and take

So,

When you come to me with nothing but a badge

And an attitude

You give me no option but to take what's mine

My respect

Singing "ISO cell ain't cold enough"

" 24 hours ain't long enough"

But my respect and integrity will last a lifetime

Especially when it is earned

These Walls Speak

-

Eyes surfing thru the walls in intake

Waiting days now for classification

Reading the story of my room thru the bricks on the wall

All the many souls left behind thru scribbles, graffiti and scars

Names left behind as if not to lose their place in history

Fallen soldiers remembered thru a barrage of RIP stamps

Eyes staring down on me

The walls are always watching

Artist with the ability to capture the very essence of a woman

Leave visual aids

Mostly for those waiting for reception

The screams from my celly tells a story of what 23-hour lockdown can do to you mentally after 6 months

Me

I'm cool as the air conditioner they leave on 24/7

Circulating the stale putrid air

Just reading the legacy on the wall

Everything from love letters to apologies

Ever heard the expression "if these walls could talk"

Well mine do

And the story of war in it is so vivid

It paints a silhouette of the battlefield

Resembling that of a roman coliseum

Although these wars are fought in a
concrete jungle

These walls just capture the story

If you can read between the lines

Thru the cracks the peels and the
chipped paint

You too can hear the stories

GONE

Found out today I lost a friend

I receive the news too late

I won't even be able to say good bye

She went in her sleep

I guess that is a blessing

But tell that to the 3 kids she left behind

Beautiful she was

And for eternity now she will be

Really can't compare her to another

The last time I seen her we laughed for hours

Before we parted I told her I love her

We were friends for now

Our time had Passed a long time ago

Her first kids father was a friend of mine

So, you know how this story goes

We were tight for a while

But as we grew the winds of change drifted us far apart

That night in the car she told me

She told me I always held a special spot in her heart

Our eyes seemed to make love in the moonlight

Trying to maintain our composure

She would try and glance away

Then she would hit the D'usse

And the inhibitions she had would fade away

In my mind she was perfect

In my site

If no one else's

All the attributes a man could want

An angel here on earth

Maybe that's why God carried her off

On the bottom bunk of this 2-man cell

My heart skipped a beat like a stutter

Reminiscing on the last words she told me

"You know I love you more, and always have"

This was her reply

When I told her that I loved her

We could blame It on the alcohol, but the truth is sobering

A long hug to solidify a decade of

feelings

Innocent was our embrace

As she went on her way I hop in my car and float away

I found out I lost a friend today

But at least she knew I loved her

Silence Speaks So Loud

Florescent lights and toothpaste

All I notice as I look up

Make shift adhesive keeping memories over head

A single picture says 1000 words

Tension in the air so thick you can cut it with a butter knife

The silence speaks so loud

War chiefs meet on the battlefield to discuss peace

Common ground is met but the soldiers refuse to sleep

So now here we lay

No one daring to say a word

But the silence speaks so loud

35 men from all walks of life crammed
together like sardines

Different cars carry us far apart, but we
never leave to dorm

The lines are invisible but we all see
them clear as day

Guards being paid to babysit

Not enough of them to prevent the
clash of these titans

All under the same oppression

But still we single each other out

Disrespectful slurs being whispered in
dark corners

But the silence speaks so loud

I close my eyes and open wide my ears

Sleep is a luxury we experience very
lightly

If at all

Up by 4 am again

Ready to program for another day

Ready to pop of at a moment's notice

But for now,

We speak of peace

But the silence speaks so loud

Edible Auction Block

"Cold tray for hot tray"

"Peanut butter for cereal"

Yells from the mess hall in the breakfast line

Deals being dealt by men as if on the floor on Wall Street

"2 breads for a milk"

"Hot and cold tray for a soup"

Using the barter system, the best way we know how

In an attempt to find satisfaction

From this slop we are forced to eat

"Waffy for jelly"

"Meat and taters for cold tray and juice"

Herding us to the door as we make way for the next rush

"Sir you can't take that orange out of here"

In an attempt to keep us men sobered up

"Sir you can't fill your cup with water"

"You have to use the cups we give you"

Trying to taste a full cup of water that is cold

Without the slight hint of rust from old pipes

And this shit came from a garden hose

But to my mouth this is as fresh as a glacier from the Alps

Urine still dark even though water is all we drink

And you can't blame it on my choice of diet

Because with no money on my books this is all I eat

Guards watching us put toxins in our bodies

They wouldn't even feed to the family pet

Forgetting we men are human beings but somehow,

They demand respect

Maybe we should complain

Write a petition

Do a strike

But then

We hear they brought in 69 more inmates just last night

Not trying to be back on lockdown

Or even worse

In the hole with fecal matter dried on the floors

Pepper sprayed and stripped past my drawls

Like cheap dope fiend whores

1000 push-ups a day and still powerless to fight back

"Line up for chow gentlemen"

Its lunch time so we march on back

"Cold tray for bologna"

"Kool aid for a orange"

Back to the edible auction block we go

After eating this shit all year

I better not come to this bitch no more

R U Ready

Sacrifice and the days of humiliation

We created a maze of contradictions

Strange fruit use to be hanging

Now they just store it away

In prison cells wasting time and spoiling away

Cover the heart with a look of unconcern

Use to wait in line waiting to get our turn

For equality, stability, respect and reparation

But glory is not for the giving

Glory is for the taking

Separation was a tool to leave us

helpless

Needing to come together like the beads on a necklace

Younger generations got the power and the platform

Elders got all the knowledge

Man, what else can we ask for

History is made just by taking action

Sometimes ain't no talking needed to really get it cracking

Long as we all agree what we are fighting for

All these lost comrades show us what we are fighting for

Kids in the street watching time just pass

O.G.'s scared to leave the past in an hour glass

"It's nation time"

That's what they was yelling

Our teachers are dying

But are we keeping the lesson

These hands right here they do for self

We handle our business not begging for help

A leader was born and I'm preparing myself

But my elders taught me first I can't do it by myself

Can't solve our problems with the same thinking we use to create them

Our old habits didn't work so it's time to replace them

I live as a soldier,

But I'll die as a legend

Now who's coming with me

That's the question

-

-
-

-

Forgiveness

-

Forgiveness is never easy

It's a tough pill to swallow

Eyes glazed with the memory of yester year

Putting a mirror to your own insecurities

Finding faults in others around me that have crossed my line of comfort

Post traumatic syndrome leaving me cold in the chest and hot in the head

Begging to reach the other side of bad intentions

Cob webs where my heart use to be

Am I still a slave?

To my thoughts

And my ability to accept how is

As a man I give respect and demand mine to the fullest

But people press your buttons like a new game controller

Seeing which ones move you

Am I wrong to put a demo out?

Feeling as if no action is a bigger crime

Or maybe I am still sick

Sick with ills of an underprivileged youth

Forced to grow in a jungle with no instruction manual

Learning what it takes to be a man

Following other misguided boys

The blind leading the blind

In a way leaving my own seeds

Out in this same jungle

Out in the cold

Perpetuating the same pain on them I cried for as a child

So, when I speak of forgiveness I speak of forgiving myself

Believing being grown means never having to say you're sorry

Even if the victim I hurt stares me in the face daily

Should I be forgiving to my trespasser
when he torments my inner peace

Should I turn the other cheek when
I'm attacked by a person I protect

Is it worth teaching when you feel the
student will never learn

Or do you look yourself in the eye and
say I forgive you

And we will walk this road together

Either that or fight it out

Until only one of us lives in this body

Hard living in a world so cruel

So, use to taking advantage of
weakness

For now,

I know which one wins

At least till I come home

For now,

Forgiveness will have to wait until
repenting is reasonable

Until then

Don't bother me

I'm in my zone

Mightier Then the Sword

The pen is mightier than the sword

Especially when jammed into exposed flesh

Nothing comes to a sleeper but a dream

But uprising brings peace to the unrest

Respect existence or expect resistance

Pushing the envelope to the law makers and officials

These real eyes

Realize

Real lies

Although my third eye is blinded a little

Never went to class but an advocate of

knowledge

I wonder if that is a parody

As a kid I begged to be in the streets

Now my kids beg for PlayStation and Xbox

Guns drugs and crime

Are broadcasted on Facebook Live

We are the ones to tell the world our true story

The sidewalk talks

In a dialect hidden from most ignorant to the sound

You just need to tune in and listen

Channel your frequency

Fostering delinquency

But fratricide is different from genocide

My uncle said the best thing he could teach me is to always pay attention

He ain't ever lied

Common sense just ain't that common

Forgive and forget left yesterday

My goal

From now til the end of eternity

Is to make tomorrow better then yesterday

Everyday

Inner Artist

Paint covers the hood of my skull

My inner artist wants to come out and play

Drawing figurines and landscapes of whimsical places

Painting emotion over the disarray

Nothing is ever simple in the mind of a maniac

His genius is too abstract

Placing jazz diction over science fiction

Or a Hip Hop beat over pure fact

Never sleep but living my dream in full HD

High definition becomes a double

entendre

Bringing back that comfortable feeling

Like soul food on Sunday with grandma

Never on a ride to get somewhere

Just a passenger blindfolded digging the sounds

The smells the voices of all the people around

My inner artist is always at work

Overtime, double time and so on and so forth

Every experience feeds him more

Watch as he lifts his sleeves and grabs his fork

Giving over to the feeling of being free

My inner artist is the best part of me

Warrior Mind Set

Unhealthy is my mindset

Not because I plan to do wrong

Not because I have an underlying addiction I don't know about

Not because I have deep seeded issues imbedded from childhood

Or have malicious intent

My mindset is unhealthy because I am not comfortable within myself to stand on my decisions

I was taught you are a man of your word when your No Means No and your Yes Means Yes

Well what about my maybes

Or my sometimes thinking

The "depending how I feel" approach

Values, morals and ethics

That stands for a lot

Depending on the circumstance

How often do we surround ourselves with contradictions?

Lying to ourselves just long enough to not hurt someone else's feelings

Self-deception is the worst kind

How can you demand consistency but fail to lead through action?

Maybe

You not as solid as you thought

You may not break, but you do tend to bend sometimes

Afraid to be uncomfortable

But that's the time you really grow

Sounds like self-sabotage to me

Foul is the friend who refuses to tell you you're doing it all wrong

If I'm willing to watch you fail

That means I never had love for you in the first place

In a world of politically correct

An orange is still an orange

We lose our battles, not by refusing to fight

But by switching up the reason we fight for

Never perfect but always honest is the path to redemption

Every journey begins one step at a time

But what about the time we waste just dancing in circles

Walking dumb never consequence thinking

Is your means to an end what you want your end to mean?

Before I check your solidification, the mirror is my soap box

Pulling my inner soldier out of his comfort zone

Letting him know it's a war outside

And the future of my kids hangs I the balance

Fuck everybody else this is a personal challenge

Blood has already been shed and prisoners of war have been taken

I feel the enemy getting closer

But I can't move how I want if I'm not clear what I'm thinking

The time has come for me to agree to say fuck our feelings

Are you with me or not

If not, you will be left behind

The first battle to win is inside our mind

If there is no enemy inside, then the one outside can't touch me

But before you can follow me I need to know that I can trust

Me

-

-
-

-
-

-
-

-

TIME

For certain I know that time is a constant

If all we have is time

Than wouldn't it be worth more than monetary gain

Certainly, we are born to die

As air first enters our body as a new born

Out comes our first scream of horror

We were born with only 2 fears

The fear of falling

And loud unidentifiable noise

All other fears are learned

Fear of rejection

Which in turn forces you to augment your own reflection

The fear of heights

Which subconsciously redirects your direction

The fear of death

Which undoubtedly hinders your perception

My inner spirit animal is a phoenix

Who must die to be reborn

Arising from the ashes

Bigger, better, faster and stronger

Born to fly,

But often hunted to be captured

Only to be seen by people that may never understand me

Not to be confused with other chickens and turkeys

I know that as I fail I am ultimately succeeding

I have erased the bars placed on me by society

The stipulations of being a kept citizen

No

I don't live in that world anymore

Living in that place of "Oh woe is me"

Helpless only helps in fairytales

But all the heroes must fight the dragons

The journey is long and hard

But that's why it is spoken about for centuries

Sung from the lips of men and women too scared to find their own adventure

If you never venture off the beaten path you end up walking in circles

Or unknowingly giving yourself limitations to your existence

Me

I would rather be a rebel

A prince turned pauper turned prisoner turned soldier

To unanimously become king

Weeds grow in my backyard with no need to tend to

They come in all seasons

Waiting to choke the life out of dreams starting to blossom

Kill the roots and rot the fruit

There are few tongues I understand

But grief was one I spoke fluently

Spoken by all that were around me

Almost in a way to glorify it

I say the buck stops here

I am rewriting this story

Time starts now

Prepping My People

We all sit around as our rights are being taken away in our face

Powerless is not a feeling strong people find common

But that

Plus, hopeless joyless and a gang of other lesses fill our subconscious

Fear for the future due to lack of consolidation

I was told proper preparation prevents poor performance

Now a days these 5 p's penetrate my psyche

Passing thru problems plaguing the people past and present

Me

I'm just popping my p's on another page

Being wide awake but still paralyzed in the process of progress

I don't know about you, but I slept thru the inauguration

Now I awaken to a world of total uncertainty

Being Muslim is a crime

Which as I was told is translated only to mean servant of God

The separation begins

I waited to see what would happen when being Mexican becomes a crime

Too late

The biggest crime is being poor in a place of privilege

Where the prison population never plummets

And police pummel pedestrians to a pulp in public and private places

These days I pray for peace

And prepare for Armageddon

Reaching a hand out to comrades on this battle ground

This time the war is being televised

The war is for our minds

The war is for our children

The war is for our freedom that they hide thru this high tech, multi pixeled 1000 channel brain washer

That a lot of us parents

Use as a designated babysitter

We must get back to the basics on whole new level

Military muscle is being replaced by gamers

Cars drive themselves

And in the attempt to make our lives a little easier

We willingly gave away all our privacy

Sucks when you iPhone requires a fingerprint

Making our phones so smart we

become stupid

The world is at our fingertips, yet we still argue over social media post

Time to clear the smoke

And realize just how far down the rabbit hole you truly went Alice

Let's remember why we do what we do

Let's remember what it takes to be free

Let's stop worrying about the future so much we forget to live and fix the issues of the present

Let us prepare…

For our preservation

As a people

Time (Passing Us By)

Push-ups, dips, burpees, squats

The things we do to pass the time

Pinochle, spades, dominoes, chess

Read and gamble to cloud our minds

Read more in a week then I did in a year

Eyes scroll lines with words on the paper

Orange or grape

Lemon or punch

We form concoctions for food options that would amaze the masses

You'd be surprised the things you can create

With noodles, chips, beans and Kool

aid packets

Beef jerky, a bag of rice and you can feed 10 people

Tortilla shells chili and cheese

Not the kind you cut

But the kind you squeeze

Whole bunch of starch in this bag of mine

Don't know what I be eating half the time

But right now, it tastes like the finest cuisine

Turn on the television to watch your favorite team

Or maybe some Maury to see who's the daddy

War stories about outside is a normal thing sadly

Some say who they are

Others say who they are not

Some constantly go to the penitentiary

Some been stabbed or shot

Some got short time some got a lot

Some sleep on the street some be on the block

The one thing we all have in common is time

Time to do and time to kill

Time changes some of their lives for the better

Or they find new and improved ways to fuck up their lives still

Time

The one thing in life you can't get back

These men up in here invented a lot of things

But no one found a way to bring back that

Years wasted

Relationships crushed

Only now realizing they needed or loved certain people so much

News flashes show warm bodies that are now cold to the touch

Ashes to ashes

Dust to dust

Hurry up and wait

That's the name of the game

Some rush to the phone

Others learn to or continue to pray

Some shoot the shit others take time to

think

Finding something useful they can take away

Pull ups, crunches, more push-ups and dips

As we find ways to pass the time away

Love Meant for You

The love that was meant for you

Was never meant to be

It has been a long long time

And I remember when my name was written on your binder

And on you heart

Never did I give you a third of what you gave to me

And I noticed

That I may be the reason you became afraid to love

Experimenting trying to find yourself

Thru lies you had to tell yourself

Getting high so when people ask you how you are doing

You reply by saying "I'm feeling myself"

But I want to apologize for what my 14-year-old self had done to you

Not knowing your lack of self-worth came way before me

I was just the straw that broke the camel's back

If I had a time machine I would take it all back

Tell you how beautiful you are

And how afraid I was to feel love

Because when you feel born to lose you also become afraid to win

If I could only see you again

I would wipe away the tears I caused

Sending a butterfly effect flipping thru time like Dominique Dawes

I never wanted to be the one to magnify your flaws

And I ask you to forgive me

Being a man with 2 daughters I could never imagine them so empty

The visuals over social media say plenty

But I just want that 14-year-old girl to know

In my eyes you are beautiful to me

WAKE UP

Wake up

Dream land beckons and your bed seems heavenly

But, wake up

You are in a warm box of familiarity

But, wake up

You are free as a bird in a sky with no end in sight

But, wake up

You are limitless in a sea of color as your imagination takes flight

But, wake up

The cars, the jewels, the clothes and the status seem so real

But, wake up

You engulf yourself in the high you

get and how good you feel

But, wake up

As you turn you awaken to the reality
you are laying on cold steel

You wake up

To a reality in front of you that you
wish wasn't real

Wake up!!!

-

-

IN THIS ROOM

-

The room I am in is small

Trapped in the corner

Originally intended for a child

Toys in the corner taking up space

Pallet on the floor with the stale scent

of Newport 100's

Walk in closet with no room to take a step

Dingy brown carpet which is soft to the feet yet bad for the lungs

Television on a dinner tray

Chipped paint on chocolate brown trimming

With a lock on top of the door to keep someone out

Or better yet lock someone in

Pallet on the shared by a family lost and left abandoned

Child raised by grandpa's girlfriend because mommy wants nothing to do with her

The smell of burnt cigarettes mask the scent of meth in their pores

Chipped paint on the chocolate trimming in the doorway lack care

Paint been in this house longer then the residence

But no one seems to care

"They just keep passing me by"

Never once taking a second glance

Of the scars that lie over head

Paint chips falling on toys left in a pile against the wall

Meant for joy but very seldom heard laughter

Dolls enduring the abuse the child witnessed between mommy and daddy

When you ask the baby why Barbie must go to the hospital

And the child explains "because she didn't listen to daddy"

And grabs the nerf gun as a brief intermission

Can you see the story playing out in this baby's brain?

So, clear it holds a place in this game

The lock on the door is for the monster in the room

To keep all the bad things locked in

Or when granddad and his girlfriend are getting high

Old as the house itself it seems

Out dated but with a usefulness til this day

Lock in the monster

Protect the baby

Or is the baby the monster

The skeletons trapped in the closet so packed no one will find them

Let alone a sock or a bracelet

All this room filled with anguish

Story after story of unwanted things
shoved away for no one to see

But that doesn't mean it isn't there

So much pain in such a small room

Health Care

Footsteps pound the ground

And the sound of machines beeping

Nurses strolling from room to room

Pain and anguish on so many faces

Over crowded

There are no more beds

Code blues and body alarms going off

Pain in the air

So many people came with ailments

Physical mental and emotional

So many people to care for that the people running the facility view you as a number

For now, this is C-7

Been here 6 hours and still no diagnosis

Wheels squeaking the linoleum floors

Key cards opening double wedged doors

They gave pain meds but there is still a need for more

So many people

But yet you can still feel so alone

Good news

We have a bed open for you

In this room and the constant beep of this machine is my sanctuary

No visitors to speak of per se

Just an onsite nurse doing rounds

So silent you can hear crocs clear as church bells from down the hall

Trapped in your own thoughts while the machine keeps beeping

Blood pressure taken sporadically is a healthy change in rhythm

The music of the emptiness

No chance to see a change

White wall and bed pans

Food tray and a garbage can

Guess sleep is the most logical option

Feeling so alone you speak to yourself

But those conversations aren't always so pleasant

Upper D Men

Its early in the am

And the sun has yet to kiss the morning sky

We,

The Upper Demons

Are awake and alert

Tensions are high as men of valor suit up for the morning activities

We are ever vigilant and ready for action

Quoting loud enough for anyone to hear

"Respect the organization or the organization will give a demonstration"

The doors pop

Marching like gladiators on our way to a Roman arena

Not too sure what lays ahead

But too active to even care

As we reach our destination we swarm in like angry wasp

Or more like a pack of hyenas urging to attack

Sniffing out our prey

The room is met with a thunderous roar as lightning strikes

Again, and again, and again

Until now

We feel the point has been made

Mission accomplished as we mingle back into the daily routine

Doors pop again, and we reassemble

All demons accounted for

Back into our cage

Back into the darkness

Back into the black hole

Nothing can touch us in our circle

Emerging victorious

We,

The Upper Demons

Creep back into our pits and fall asleep

Powerful and assured

To most this is hell

But for us

It's just another day

No Remorse

The things you do become an imprint on your life

Your soul can be blemished from split second decisions

No one can judge a man fully until you know the dark places he's chosen to dwell

The pits of hell boil over unleashing demons onto this world

Plaguing the weakest minded of us

Sexual deviants searching for prey

The torment must be unbearable for someone like that

What ugliness must a man have?

To find sexual pleasure from a child

Sickness is how they describe it

I was also told when water no longer works

Fire gets everything clean

Me having daughters, a sister, and a mother I love dearly

Forgive me if I feel death is too easy for this crime

Innocence is like time

Once you lose it you never get it back

How weak do you have to be to find power in taking something so pure

A man died yesterday

And not one tear was shed on my side

The price paid in blood felt justified in the eyes of us men

Us men of morals, standards and integrity

No man can judge but God

And let he without sin cast the first stone

But as he prayed for forgiveness on the inside someone felt it was time to send him home

He probably in his heart never felt so alone

And wishes he could take it back deep down in his bones

Bludgeoned so hard you could hear the pain from his moans

But fuck that

I don't program with rapist or child molesters

I have taken many thigs

But the things I chose to take can be replaced

Taking advantage of small weaker people in my mind makes you a coward

Starring down from your glass tower

Feeling you are safe

But as the people destroy your tower

You fall helplessly on your face

You can find my sympathy in the dictionary

Between shit and syphilis

I am no judge, so I can offer no sentence

But the torcher you feel deep down should be endless

Matter of fact

Let me pray God has mercy on your soul

And the demon that possessed you be cast into a deep dark hole

Down so deep air can't even find it

He could lie with his mouth, but his eyes couldn't hide it

To all the kids that have ever been molested

To the women who said "NO" and their cries were neglected

To the men whose manhood at some point was tested

A man died yesterday

And not one tear was shed on my side

No one can judge a man fully until you know the dark places he's chosen to dwell

But fuck that

I don't program with rapist or child molesters

Christmas Blues

Waking up to a cold dark sky

And all I notice is a single star

Moon leaving a thumb nail stamp in the corner

While traces of indigo blankets the bottom of this starless sky

Sun rise is just around the corner

It's about 32 degrees

And the chill from the night air does the same job as a strong cup of coffee

But honestly, I'd rather be dreaming

Dreaming of aerosol snow flurries Christmas lights and the smell of fresh pine

The laughter of joy after a few sips of

wine

Or maybe some egg nog with brandy

But mostly the joyful faces of children

Rushing me with love and excitement

Feeling more blessed then a millionaire could understand

With just a sprinkle of gold glittering across their cheerful glances

"Daddy, daddy look at this"

"Wow, cool thank you daddy thank you"

The present I have under the tree is little bodies ripping paper in an anxious frenzy

And for me

That's all I need to be happy

A single kiss from the woman I adore

A call from my mother and sister and even my father

A text from my folks "Merry X-mas Don"

Simple as it sounds I will miss all this

For now, it can only be a dream

My home for now is covered in barbwire

With several guards patrolling the scene

"Merry Christmas gentlemen, now make it back to the house"

You mean the dorm where I sleep on this hard ass bunk

With no refrigerator, like 40 other men and no couch

"Aite, I'll be in in a minute"

That's my only reply

For now, I gaze into this 1-star sky

The sound of O.G.'s on the phone with their grandchildren

Trying to keep family ties with people they may not see in a while

Life is what you make it I guess

Reminiscing with my fellow brothers in blue on what we will miss

As I stare thru the bars on my window

Colors transfer to baby blue and cotton candy pink

The rest of the dorm is wide awake

But me I'm about to go back to sleep

With my county issued jacket as a pillow

I rest my weary head

Staring at a steel bunk in a cold uncomfortable bed

I am thankful to be alive

Because next year it will be alright

But for now, let me fall into this comma

Merry Christmas to all and to all a good night

www.ingramcontent.com/pod-product-compliance
Lightning Source LLC
Chambersburg PA
CBHW020019050426
42450CB00005B/543